THE SOLACE SWING

Jette Steen

The Solace Swing

Jette Steen

1. Edition

2013

Published by Jette Steen F/F

ISBN: 978-87-995750-3-9

Copyright © JS-2013

The Solace Swing

DEDICATION

With thanks to Siggi Forberg for translation.

Preface

The idea for this story arose by the thought of a short old urban legend about this topic.
I think it was called "The Dead Child in the Baby Bouncer".
You may recognize that part of the tale, but the rest is quite a different and extended story and pure fiction.

Chapter 1

On this particular spring morning their home is humming with activity. Gitte is to be married and everything must be perfect. Her mother, Inga, is tidying up the kitchen while her father, Konrad, is reading his paper in the sunroom when Gitte rushes down the stairs from the second floor.

She sits down beside her father and has a glass of juice and quickly eats a toast. Konrad looks at Gitte above his glasses:

"What a hurry."

Gitte gives him a great smile.

"Yes, I´ve got a lot of things to attend to. I must be at the hairdresser´s in half an hour."

"You need not go to the hairdresser´s today; Jesper won´t be able to recognize you."

Konrad gives her an arch smile while Inga who has also entered the sunroom smiles at her daughter and says.

"Yes, of course you do. Especially on this day it is important to feel like the most beautiful girl in the world."

Gitte gets up and in no time she is in the hall shouting "See you" and then she disappears.

Inga is smiling to herself.

"It is a great day for Gitte and Jesper. Do you remember our wedding day? Who would think it´s more than thirty years ago."

"No, but we have had our ups and downs, but today when we look back we´ve been doing quite well."

Konrad turns to his paper again and Inga clears the rest of the table and returns to the kitchen.

Well, yes, he´s right. Things have gone our way. Inga remembers the first time after their wedding. They hadn´t got a bean, but Inga had become pregnant and there was no doubt that they were to marry before the state of affairs was obvious.

Konrad was employed with a large textiles company and at the same time he studied to complete his MBA; so they didn´t always spend so much time together as she wanted when Gitte was a baby.

When Gitte started school Inga had a part-time job at a lawyer´s office which she liked very much until the firm was handed over to a character she absolutely did not like.

But, luckily, Konrad had been doing very well and when he took over the textiles company they agreed that the best thing would be for her to become a stay-home wife.

"Are you just lost in your own thoughts?"

Inga starts when Konrad is suddenly standing in front of her.

"Oh yes, and I didn´t hear you coming."

Konrad hugged his wife.

"You women are so romantic and I bet you were thinking of when we were married."

"Yes, and you men think you know everything."

She smiles.

"But shouldn´t you go over your speech once more while Gitte is out?"

A few hours later Gitte rushes through the door again.

"Well, what do you think?"

Both Konrad and Inga smile while they´re looking at their daughter and telling her how beautiful she is before Gitte rushes upstairs.

A moment later the doorbell rings. It is the delivery man from the florist´s with the table decorations and the wedding bouquet.

Shortly after the doorbell rings again and Gitte´s friend, Vibeke, is standing outside looking excited. She hurries up the stairs to Gitte.

Inga goes into the large dining room to lay the table.
Soon after Malene, who has promised to assist in the kitchen arrives.

Inga shows her into the dining room where the table is laid for 14 persons. Malene admires the decorations which are very impressive and everything looks beautiful. Then they go out into the kitchen where Inga tells Malene what to do.

Malene makes some open sandwiches and lays the table in the kitchen while Inga goes upstairs to have a shower. She can hear Gitte and Vibeke laughing so she knocks on the door and enters Gitte´s room to make sure that all is well.

The two friends are still giggling while they reassure Inga that everything is as it should be. Giggling again they say they were just lost in memories of old boyfriends and, shaking her head, Inga tells them that lunch is almost ready and then she goes to have her shower.

A little later they are all gathered in the kitchen and Konrad notices Gitte´s make-up. He smiles and asks Vibeke.

"Where did you learn to do that kind of full war paint?"

Gitte immediately defends her friend.

"Vibeke is used to seeing that even the greatest artists look right. She has even done make-up on ...."

Inga interrupts.

"I really think it is beautiful and don´t mind an old man´s comments when it comes to beauty."

Gitte doesn´t eat very much, but quickly gets up from the table and hurries upstairs again and Vibeke immediately follows her.

Inga who is wearing her bathrobe also goes upstairs to dress observing that Konrad has not yet had a bath. He gets up murmuring that it won´t take long for him to be diked out.

Only when the horse-drawn carriage was ready outside Konrad shouts.

"Inga, have you seen my cufflinks?"

Inga shrugged despairingly.

"I told you they are beside your script."

Vibeke who had also changed comes down into the hall where Inga compliments her good looks and they are standing together watching Gitte coming down the stairs in her fancy dress.

Inga joins her hands saying.

"Gee how beautiful you are, young lady."

Konrad is also looking at her with great satisfaction.

Malene and Vibeke help Gitte arranging her dress in the carriage which Konrad has also entered and then Inga and Vibeke get into a taxi which then leaves for the church.

Jesper and his brother Philip welcome them and Inga gives Jesper a big hug while she smiles knowingly.

"Now you are very soon a married man, Jesper."

"Yes, it´s a nice thought."

Jesper smiles at her and puts one of his arms around her.

"However, you´ll still see your daughter very often once we´ve moved into the little house."

Jesper looks at the verger and beckons Philip after which they hurry into the church and soon after Inga follows suit.

The music begins and in through the door the bride comes with her beautiful wedding bouquet arm in arm with her father.

A few hours later the guests are dining and chatting in a cheerful atmosphere.

Looking at Philip Konrad asks.

"Your turn, I guess?"

Philip shakes his head.

"No, I really don´t think so. I will have to find her first and I don´t think there are many girls who want to marry me as long as I travel so much as I do. But maybe if I´ll find one in Africa."

"Well, do you plan to continue working with "Doctors without Borders"?"

"So far, I think it´s important and I feel good about it. But surely I will settle down some day."

He looks at his brother and continues.

"It´s a pity, that my parents did not live to experience this day."

Konrad looks at him solemnly.

"Yes, how long time is it since they died?"

Philip frowned thoughtfully.

"Well, it´s one year and a half since they died. Strange to think that if they had missed the plane then it would not have happened."

"Well yes, you never know what fate has in store for you. One might live to be a hundred, but one might also drop dead tomorrow. It´s a good thing that we don´t know..."

Jesper interposes.

"Don´t you both look so serious. Cheers."

Jette Steen

Chapter 2

A few months later Gitte and Jesper, sounding the horn of their car, are pulling into the driveway of Inga´s and Konrad´s house. They get out and walk into the house as Jesper is shouting.

"Anybody here for a weekend getaway?"

Inga is walking down the stairs carrying a weekend bag and Konrad is making sure that all doors and windows are securely locked while shouting from the sunroom.

"So, you are already here?"

Jesper carries the baggage in the hall out into the trunk of his station wagon and eventually Konrad is turning up with a fishing rod which is carefully put into the trunk.

Jesper closes the trunk, they both get into the front seats and the car starts.

A few hours later they are standing in front of the cosy cabin which Konrad got rather cheap many years ago. It is situated right in the middle of a small wood only about a kilometer from the beach.

They have used it at all times of the year and every time the family have needed some peace and tranquillity. Konrad hurries inside to light the fireplace while the others bring in the baggage.

Inga has brought a stew and she hurries to lay the table and serve the food after which they chat quietly in the dimmed light from the candles and a few kerosene lamps.

Konrad and Jesper spend the next few days fishing. They compete and proudly show their catch to Inga and Gitte who duly praise them when they are not making use of the freedom to take long walks or read.

Inga tells Gitte that she had had a mammography and therefore she has an appointment at the hospital Monday next. Gitte looks solemnly at her.

"What is going to happen?"

"Well, I think it's just a matter of some tests and blood samples. In fact I don't know and I don't want to think about it."

But already Monday Inga undergoes an operation for breast cancer. Konrad tells Gitte on the phone. He picks her up and together they go to see her mother at the hospital.

Gitte notices that her mother is not feeling well.

"That certainly went fast. When did they tell you that they wanted to operate on you?"

Inga gives Gitte an apologetic glance.

"Well, they did say that they might operate on me today, but then again they might not so there was no reason to be restless, was there?"

During the following weeks Inga has radiotherapy and chemotherapy and gradually she loses her hair and she is in low spirits. Poor Konrad is deeply concerned.

Jesper and in particular Gitte very often drop in to help with this and that and Gitte almost does all their shopping for them. And several times a week she and

Jesper come round to cook together in her parents´ kitchen which is quite a new thing for Konrad who has never boiled as much as an egg.

But now he finds it rather cosy and nice and has begun to interfere. Gitte puts him to work and then they have a drink while sharing the work and as Konrad puts it, it all gets better by that.

One afternoon when Gitte is taking time off to counterbalance overtime she decides to pick up Inga who is now wearing a scarf so no-one can see that she has lost her hair.

Gitte stops at a small milliner´s and in the shop Inga notices that they also stock wigs. She and Gitte had been talking about a wig for her and she is surprised to see the wide range in the shop.

She finds one which might as well be her own hair as it was before the operation and that lifts her spirits. She tries it on and insists on wearing it at once.

Then they have lunch and buy new clothes and when they get home Konrad notices that she is pleased and at once says,

"Wow, you look great."

Inga gives him an arch smile.

"Yes, don´t I? I do hope I can get used to wearing it."

Konrad goes out into the kitchen where he was peeling potatoes and cooking pointed cabbage in white sauce. Inga is astonished.

"You must have been home early Konrad since you have managed to do some shopping and all."

"Well, no, I must admit that I got Jytte to do the shopping for me when she had an errand at lunch time. She also told me how to cook pointed cabbage in white sauce."

Konrad puts the meat in the frying pan.

"I am going to fry some pork chops for the cabbage. Doesn´t that sound good?"

"Oh, yes, It certainly sounds great."

Konrad turns round to look at her.

"By the way, she also sends her regards."

A few moments later Gitte and Jesper arrive, sit down and look in admiration at Konrad´s well-laid table and everybody praises his delicious food. Gitte raises her glass with red wine and looks inquiringly at her father.

"Now, I suppose you have not had a drink when cooking the food today since you were all alone?"

Konrad nodded.

"Yes, you bet I have. Now that you´ve ruined me why shouldn´t one have a drink even if one is alone?"

Jesper and Gitte laugh.

While they are eating Konrad tells them that he is planning to sell his company. He has long thought that it was time to step down and let some new people take over.

"Niels has been with me longer than anybody else and he knows how to do things, so I think I´ll ask him if he wants to take over."

"But do you think he can afford it?" Inga frowns.

"Of course, I´ve thought about it and the possibility that he can just manage the business instead of me, but I don´t know .... We´ll got to wait and see; I have a meeting with my accountant tomorrow and there we´ll be talking about it."

A week later Gitte and Jesper go for a ski vacation in France.

One of the days snow is drifting so heavily that when they are getting off the lift Gitte cannot orientate herself. She stumbles and falls farther down than expected.

At first she looks startled then she gives Jesper a radiant smile and begins to get up, but as she gets up her skis slide backwards and within seconds she slides down the hill at full speed.

Jesper hurries down to where Gitte is lying crying. He comforts her as best he can and is trying to help her get up, but realizes that it was a severe fall so he sends for help and soon after the ambulance arrives. They go to the hospital where the doctors find that her leg is broken.

When Gitte returns to Denmark a couple of days later with her leg in a cast she moves into her old room at Inga and Konrad´s because Jesper is going on a business trip. Inga enjoys getting the chance to fuss over Gitte. She spoils her and they have a nice time together.

About a week after Jesper has come home Konrad has back pain because he had cleaned an eaves gutter and Jesper asks him to leave that sort of thing to him in future.

Afterwards Konrad amuses them for a long time telling them how things are concerning the handover of the business.

"But a good thing that I discussed it with my accountant:"

The others glance at him with questioning smiles on their faces and he continues.

"He happened to know one who would very much like to carry on the business and after all Niels couldn´t afford it. A pity that I mentioned it to him, but I think he will get along very well with Lars."

Jesper laughs.

"Yes, and of course you´ve got a reasonable price, I imagine. But what then?"

Konrad smiles at him.

"Well, I´m going to cook, e.g. fried pork and parsley sauce."

Inga laughs out loud and Konrad continues.

"Well, naturally I will be at the office for the next six months, but I´ll just be counting the money and reply to this and that."

Jesper´s mobile phone rings.

"Oh, I forgot to silence my mobile; I´ll just see who´s calling!"

Jesper answers the phone.

"Hi Philip, how are you old boy? - You have? - That must have been awful. Have you found out who is behind all this?"

Jesper is talking to Philip for quite some time.

When he closes the mobile Gitte at once asks him what has happened and Jesper tells them that Philip has been the victim of a traumatic incident.

"He had gone to see a sick child. The mother was crying when he entered the hut and suddenly some of the natives got in and mugged him.

They tied him up and took his bag with all the necessary remedies and medicine. The lot, including his car keys. They even drove off in his jeep.

Fortunately, his colleagues knew where he had gone and they came to pick him up a couple of hours later. In the meantime the child´s mother had cut him loose, but there was nothing he could do for the sick child."

One Sunday afternoon a few months later Gitte and Jesper are again in her parents´ sunroom drinking coffee. Gitte gives her secret away telling her parents that she is pregnant.

The pleasure is obvious and quite overwhelmed Inga exclaims.

"Gee, imagine, we are going to be grandparents, Konrad, isn´t it wonderful?"

"Yes, I´ll look forward to it, especially now that time allows me to; it´ll be great."

They all go on chatting and look at one another in anticipation.

A little later Inga asks.

"How is Philip? Is he better now?"

Jesper shrugs.

"No on the contrary. He is very ill. He has a high fever and nobody seems to be able to find out what it is or what it takes for him to recover. I´ve told him to ask for a discharge to Denmark."

"And what does he answer?"

"He would consider it. He doesn´t want to become a burden to anybody as he puts it. But first he must go to hospital, I suppose, and then I have told him that he can stay at our place for the time being."

Now Konrad interferes.

"Out of the question with the little house you have. He can stay here in Gitte´s old room."

Inga is beaming.

"Oh yes, we´ll take very good care of him."

Jesper opens his arms.

"Well, thank you, I know, but let us wait and see how it all goes."

Gitte tells her parents that Vibeke and Thomas are getting married and that they have received an invitation for the wedding.

"They are going to be married on dad´s birthday and by then surely everybody can see that I´m pregnant and I don´t know what to wear."

Gitte and Inga go on chatting about the wedding and clothes while Konrad and Jesper go to sit down by the fireplace. Konrad had an inquiring look on his face.

"Have you thought about our little chat up in the cabin? "Would you still like to start your own business? If so, then ... Well, I have given it some thought. I think it is a great idea and I want to support you financially."

Jesper thanks him.

"Well, I´ve also worked a bit on the idea. In fact, I have found a place where five or six people can work. And then only time will show if we will need more hands. I´ve also been talking to an accountant about it."

Konrad is sipping his wine.

"Maybe we should have a word with the lawyer one of these days so that we can come up with some sensible plan. I´ll call him tomorrow."

Philip arrives in Denmark and is hospitalized for several months. When he is released he moves into Konrad and Inga´s, but he is still not well.

He begins to wet his bed and again he gets a high fever and within a couple of days he is hospitalized again. Everybody tries to help him as best they can, but apparently nothing helps and at the end Jesper is holding his hand as he passes away.

And since there is no next of kin, Jesper is busy taking care of the funeral along with a lot of practical things.

One Friday afternoon a month later Jesper and Konrad are pulling into the driveway at Strandvejen. Inside the house Inga and Gitte are waiting anxiously.

"How did it go?"

Jesper embraces Gitte.

"Beyond all expectations."

They sit down in front of the fireplace and Jesper begins telling her about the meeting with the lawyer while Inga enters the room carrying four glasses. Konrad opens a bottle of champagne and pours out.

"Congratulations and good luck, I´m sure that such a hard-working manager will succeed."

Inga raises her glass as soon as Konrad has poured out. Gitte takes her glass, too, giving an arch smile.

"Congratulations mr. Granborg, managing director."

For some time to come Jesper is very busy in his new company and he is working till late night and Inga and Konrad have gone to Majorca on vacation.

However, on September 5 the little family are gathered again because it is Inga´s birthday and also Gitte´s uncles and aunts are present.

All of a sudden Gitte gasps.

"Have you got braxton hicks again, dear?"

Inga puts her arms around her daughter. Gitte gasps again.

"In fact, I think it is more than just that. I´ve tried to count and I think there is only twelve minutes between the contractions."

Jesper phones the midwife and soon they are on their way to the hospital where Gitte gives birth to Markus almost seven hours later.

Inga and Konrad hurry to the hospital the next day. They are overwhelmed at the sight of the little boy and Inga gives Gitte a large basket full of presents and exquisite clothes some of which she herself has been knitting while Konrad gives her an envelope in which there is an advert for a fancy baby carriage and a large check.

They are talking about when Gitte and little Markus are home again and Inga who is a bit superstitious tells them that Gitte´s old cot which has been painted will not be put up until they are safely home again, but then it will be ready.

Shortly after Jesper has picked up Gitte and Markus, Konrad and Inga are standing in the doorway with the cot which is fully equipped. But they soon leave again so that the new parents can accommodate.

But it is not long before they phone to learn how things are and to offer their assistance. Markus is indeed a wished-for child they all wish to pamper and Jesper who is worked up over the new firm is grateful for their offer.

He does not want to be suffering from stress so even if Gitte might think he ought to spend more time at home everything is fine. There are no bounds as to how much Inga and Konrad want to help and even though

Gitte and Jesper sometimes feel that they would rather be alone, it is good to know that besides themselves there are some who want all the best for Markus. They manage and make the best of it all.

Jette Steen

Chapter 3

One Sunday when Markus is about six months old Jesper and Gitte go to see her parents and have their usual Sunday afternoon coffee. Konrad who has just had a cold complains of breathing difficulties and Gitte orders him to seek medical attention.

The next day Inga phones Gitte to tell her that Konrad has had a stroke and has been hospitalized. She hurries to the hospital where her mother looks despaired while Gitte tries to get an overview of the situation.

The chief physician tells them to go home as the doctors cannot do more until they have assessed the situation the next morning. Gitte picks up her mother early next morning so that they can be present at the ward round. After that they ask for a talk with the chief physician who informs them that it is all hopeless. Konrad has lost too many physical functions; he can neither speak nor move normally and soon after he passes away.

It is a terribly difficult time for Inga; fortunately for her she lives very close to Markus. She needs to feel that she is indispensable and both Gitte and Jesper give her elbow room.

Two months later Jesper, the lawyer and Inga are talking together in the sunroom and suddenly Inga says.

"Why don´t we just exchange houses? Konrad used to talk a lot about that. The young people need a large house much more than we do, he said and to be honest I don´t want to live here all alone."

A couple of months later Gitte and Jesper move into the mansion on Strandvejen. It has been painted and refurbished and Inga, who in the meantime has moved into in their small house, seems to be thriving.

Jette Steen

Chapter 4

The sun is shining beautifully on this autumn afternoon and the small provincial town shows itself in the most favourable light with a clear blue sky and the water´s quiet lap in the small harbor.

Resembling a fancy commercial on TV a large black Mercedes is moving along Strandvejen and in the car the handsome and well-dressed Jesper is sitting in the posh light yellow leather seats.

He turns up the driveway to the beautiful white mansion where he stops in front of the garage gets his leather briefcase and gets out. - Everything about him is oozing quality.

He activates the car key. Beep-beep it goes and he walks up the stairs and lets himself in through the huge main entrance on which the large polished brass door plate says "Jesper and Gitte Granborg".

Jesper goes through the high-ceilinged hall with the white wet-scrubbed walls, puts down his briefcase and then goes in through the door leading into the large beautifully decorated and designed parlor where his well-dressed mother-in-law is standing with her little grandchild in her arms.

His always elegant and beautiful wife welcomes him with a smile and a kiss.

"Hi, dad. We just figured that you might soon be home."

Smiling happily Jesper embraces her and claps her to him.

"I came as soon as I could. I mean, it's not every day one has a son who has birthday."

Jesper lets go of Gitte and reaches for Markus.

"Well what's up? Where is daddy's boy?"

Inga steps forward towards Jesper, who gives her a slight kiss on her cheek saying "hi Inga" while Inga smiles as she is handing the eager Markus to Jesper.

"Hi Jesper."

Jesper is hugging Markus and lifts him high in the air.

"Has daddy's little boy had a nice day? Have mom and granny been spoiling you?"

Markus is laughing and spitting on Jesper's tie and they all laugh.

On the floor there is a flag next to a nicely wrapped gift. Gitte takes the gift which Inga has brought and opens it and exclaims excitedly.

"Gee, is that nice, mom."

Jesper moves poking his nose impatiently so as to see.

"Let me see. What is it?"

Inga takes Markus and lift him up while she looks admiringly at him.

"Well, it´s just the brand new thing, for little boys turning one, right Markus?"

Gitte is admiring the beautifully padded baby bouncer until Jesper grabs it and goes over to stand in the doorway between the dining room and the parlor.

"Surely, it´s going to hang here?"

Gitte has an appraising look around and then she gives him a big smile.

"Yes, that will be great and then we can keep an eye on him from either rooms."

Jesper goes out into the large hall where he hangs his jacket and tie on a coat hanger.

"It´ll be exciting to put it up."

He goes outside and soon after he returns with some tools in his hand.

Meanwhile Markus has got sulky and is whimpering.

"Have a look at the roast, will you mom? Then I´ll try to calm him down."

Gitte reaches out for Markus.

"Of course dear, you take him," and then she disappears out into the kitchen while Gitte is walking about the parlor while humming a comforting tune to Markus.

A little later Jesper is standing in the middle of the doorway between the dining room and the parlor. He has a screwdriver in his hand and is looking proudly at the bouncer which he has just finished mounting.

Holding the whimpering Markus in her arms Gitte goes over to place him in the bouncer and pushes it gently so that it swings back and forth. Markus is laughing loudly while the three grown-ups are smiling and soon after Markus yawns and falls asleep.

"Well, well, dear mother-in-law. What we´re not capable of the Solace Swing can do."

They all laugh at the new term. Gitte begins laying the table while Inga and Jesper go out into the kitchen. Jesper comes with the wine and Inga comes with the food and Gitte looks inquiringly at her mother.

"Do you think I should put him into his bed? - He seems to be quite comfortable."

Inga turns to look at Markus.

"No, there is no need. He is indeed comfortable."

Looking at the sleeping kid in the bouncer Jesper gives his consent.

"Yes, no harm done considering the padded seat and then for once we can have our dinner peacefully and quietly."

They sit down at the beautifully arranged table and Jesper pours wine into the glasses and raises his glass.

"Cheers and thank you for the fine present, dear mother-in-law."

Inga takes her glass and raises it.

"Don´t mention it. Cheers and congratulations on Markus."

Gitte also raises her glass looking at Markus.

"Yes, here´s to Markus who has now turned one. I just can´t believe that a year has passed...."

Inga smiles at Gitte.

"No, but it was a good thing that your father and I just got home from Majorca. And now it´s your turn to go to Majorca. Aren´t you looking forward to it?"

Gitte frowns anxiously.

"Yes, of course, but it´s the first time I´ll be away from Markus for so long and I can hardly imagine waking up in the morning without him being there."

"But it will do you both good to have some time alone together even though I do remember how hard it was when I left you the first time."

Inga smiles as she continues.

"But I also remember how much energy I had summoned when I came home again."

"How old was I then?"

"Well, you were barely six months. You know, father had his sacred rituals...."

"Yes, he surely had and they could not be deviated from. Tell me, for how many years running did you actually go there?"

Inga thought carefully.

"Actually, it was not each and every year. We took a break for a couple of years because we went to other places and then there was the time when I was ill. In recent years we did not go anywhere."

She counts.

"But all in all we´ve been there around twenty times."

Jesper looks astonished.

"My, oh my, quite a few times."

Gitte puts down her flatware and for a while she is looking back saying absently.

"It is really weird that he´s not here anymore. Do you still miss him a lot?"

Tears came to Inga´s eyes and she blows her nose before replying sadly.

"Only almost all the time."

Jesper lifts the wine bottle over Inga´s glass.

Another glass?" and Inga apparently gets her act together and smiles.

"Yes, please."

Jesper suddenly shakes his head and seizes her by the arm.

"By the way, have you heard about this frantic businessman who left his child in his car today?"

Inga and Gitte both look anxiously at Jesper and Inga says.

"No, whatever do you mean?"

Jesper goes on saying.

"Well, I just saw it on the news before I left the office. The man was late this morning and was tearing into the parking lot at his working place.

He grabbed his briefcase and rushed out of his car and in through the door without thinking.

Left alone in the car his little daughter of a year and a half was sleeping in the back seat of the car."

Gitte looks at him in consternation.

"Oh no."

Again Jesper is gesticulating.

"But luckily one of his coworkers arrived immediately after and saw it. According to the coworker the man got somewhat embarrassed when the coworker confronted him.

He had even defended himself by saying that it was all because of stress and it was only in the last minute that it was decided that he was to take their child because his wife had been picked up by a colleague.

Therefore he had forgotten all about the child.

However, such a thing must never happen. No matter the amount of stress one should be able to remember that one has a child in the car and ...."

Gitte is shaking her head.

"Oh, how awful. Just think if his coworker had not seen it?"

"Well, don´t you think he had suddenly remembered a little later?"

Gitte gesticulates.

"Yes, but it might be rather long before he found out. And the little girl would probably wake up sooner or later.

And, can you imagine how it must be for such a little girl to wake up and find out that she is sitting all alone in the car in a strange parking lot."

"If I was his wife I would divorce him immediately. One can't be married to such an irresponsible man and father."

Inga interrupts.

"Yes, it's awful. But it's because everybody is so busy these days and people are so stressed out.

Ugh, let's forget all about that nasty story and drink to Markus. Happy birthday."

They touch glasses and Inga turns to Jesper.

"And now I need to know exactly when you are leaving."

Jesper takes the flight tickets on the sideboard behind him and turns them for Inga to see while pointing at them and Inga leans forward and reads.

"Well, then I will be here in due time before you leave."

Jette Steen

Chapter 5

One afternoon a couple of weeks later Gitte and Jesper are ready to go. The taxi is waiting in the cloudy weather in front of the impressive mansion and the trunks are ready in the high-ceilinged hall.

Little Markus is sitting in his baby bouncer in the middle of the doorway while Gitte and Jesper are mincing in the parlor and looking out the window. Jesper is scowling reproachfully at Gitte.

"What keeps her? If she doesn´t come now we´ll never make it."

"You are right and it´s really not like her. I hope nothing has happened."

Jesper looks slightly desperate as he lifts the receiver and keys Inga´s number.

Inga is standing outside the door of her small house with bags and sacks as her mobile rings.

With some difficulty she finds it in her pocket takes it and with her index finger she touches the keypad and lifts the phone to her ear.

"Hello. Yes, yes I´m on my way, but surely you are not leaving at... - What?"

Jesper is on the phone while looking out of the window.

"How far are you?"

Inga hurries out of the driveway while she is talking.

"I´m almost at the corner, I´ll be with you in half a minute."

Jesper turns around looking inquiringly at Gitte.

"Ok, mother, we´ll go outside. And we´ll leave as soon as we see you. We leave the door open and then we can talk on our way to the airport."

"Fine, have a nice trip."

"Thank you."

Jesper is quite edgy when he hangs up.

Gitte strokes the sleeping Markus´ hair and they both rush out into the driveway with their baggage and into the waiting taxi.

Gitte is looking anxiously out of the taxi´s rear window. She is relieved when she sees Inga turning the corner.

"There she is!"

Jesper, too, turns around and look out of the rear window.

"Good, now we can relax and enjoy our vacation."

The taxi starts and Gitte crosses her arms while she tries to make herself comfortable in the seat.

"Yes, Markus loves granny. They´ll have a great time together as always."

Jesper puts his hand on Gitte´s knee.

"Yea, she really dotes on the little favorite and then she´ll have something else on her mind. Apparently she misses your father a lot."

They both make themselves comfortable in the taxi which is racing to the airport.

Soon after Gitte and Jesper are running up to the check-in where they get their boarding cards at once.

They run to the exit where the stewardess is waving showing them where to go and they continue into the airplane.

Jesper makes himself comfortable and takes Gitte´s hand.

"Whew! We made it after all, one moment later and we had missed it."

They both lean back for a moment and close their eyes.

The stewardess comes up to them.

"What would you like to drink with the food?"

Gitte and Jesper give each other a meaningful look and they both say.

"Champagne, please."

They giggle as they used to when they were newly in love and take each other´s hands.

Chapter 6

Darkness and a pouring rain descend on the mansion and the sound of thunderclap is heard while flashes of lightnings are all over the sky.

The front door of the mansion at Strandvejen is half open and suddenly the shadows of two persons are approaching the front door and whispering voices are heard in the dark.

"Not a damn soul. I saw them leave by taxi with a lot of bags and trunks. They were in a hurry. They must have forgotten to lock the door."

The cone of light from a flashlight hits the walls of the hall and the TV parlor where it stops.

"It´s really pretty here."

Benny touches the remote of the large flat screen hanging on the wall in the parlor and admires the impressive paintings and artifacts.

Alex is coming down the stairs from the second floor. He goes into the parlor where Benny is turning on the light.

"No, nobody upstairs either. Not a soul."

Alex is giving Benny a knowing look.

"I´d better get the car."

Benny begins to dismantle the TV set and soon after Alex comes into the parlor again and begins to put the laptop, the digital camera and a lot of DVDs into the bag he brought along. They carry it all out into the van.

Alex turns around to face the impressive house again.

"They must have some booze in the house, too!"

Benny looks around. There is no-one and the only sound to be heard is the pouring rain where they hide at the large tree in front of the main entrance.

Alex walks up towards the house again and Benny is following him. They enter the hall and Alex continues to the open door leading into the dining room.

He goes in through the door, but immediately after he hurries out again while he is shouting.

"Let´s get out!"

Benny looks inquiringly at Alex.

"What is it?"

He goes forward to look in through the door.

In the doorway between the two rooms Markus is sleeping in the baby bouncer.

"I thought you said there was nobody here."

Quietly he tiptoes up beside Markus and looks at him carefully.

"Do you think he´s dead?"

At the same moment Markus mumbles and opens his eyes and Benny takes a step back. Alex quickly goes towards the front door and Benny runs after him while he is looking at Alex and saying.

"But we can´t just leave him?"

"What the fuck do you want us to do?"

Alex continues out through the front door while Benny rushes after him.

"Didn´t you say that they had gone on a vacation?"

"Belt up, Benny! You don´t really believe that they have let their own kid down? There must be someone in the house - or nearby. Come on we´re off."

Benny and Alex sneak to the van where they close the doors silently and off they go at full tilt.

Jette Steen

Chapter 7

Jesper is standing at a glass case in the lobby of the hotel in Majorca. He takes some brochures and goes over to Gitte who is standing at the entrance of the hotel.

They go outside where they feel the nice warm air meeting them and they continue down the street which is full of small restaurants of all ethnic origins.

They look at the many people before they decide to sit down at a table outside a Mexican restaurant where they scrutinize the menu before they order the food from the waiter.

They are hungry and they quickly eat the portion of food without saying anything after which they are having a curious look round.

A young couple are walking down the street. The two young lovers chat and laugh until they suddenly stop surprised to see Gitte and Jesper in front of them.

Thomas puts a hand on Jesper´s shoulder.

"If that ain´t? Yes, if that ain´t mister long shot himself from Denmark."

Jesper turns round and smiles broadly as he sees that it is his best childhood friend, Thomas, standing in front of him together with his wife, Vibeke. He gets up to greet them.

"Well, who would have thought that. The keeper has also found his way to the South. Hello there. Do sit down."

They all embrace and move another small table up to the table Gitte and Jesper are sitting at and they all sit down.

"How long have you been here?"

Thomas asks and Jesper tells them that they have only just arrived.

"So that´s why we haven´t met one another until now. We have been here a week and luckily we will stay this week, too."

Vibeke interrupts.

"Yes, isn´t it great to be in the South in this nice warmth. I rang home to my mother about five o´clock and she told me that it was pouring down back home and that lightning had struck the small clubhouse at the harbor."

Jesper and Gitte listen intensely and then Jesper says.

"So that´s probably why we haven´t been able to get in touch with Gitte´s mother at home. She´s looking after Markus while we´re on vacation."

Vibeke gestures.

"Yes, I guess you´re right. My mom lives right behind you."

Gitte frowns and looks worried.

"When did you speak to your mom, did you say? At five?"

Vibeke nods.

"It was about that time I tried to get in touch with my mom from Kastrup. I tried again when we had landed about eight. But I don´t understand ... I tried her mobile, too. She didn´t answer that either."

Vibeke can´t help laughing.

The Solace Swing

"Isn´t there something with your mother always forgetting to charge her mobile? I shall never forget the story you told us about when you gave her a mobile for a birthday present."

They all laugh out loud while Gitte nods and brightens and seems to calm down.

The waiter is approaching the four young people carrying a tray. They open their eyes wide and clap their hands as they see the fancy drinks and they sit for a long time laughing and chatting together.

"Now let´s party the night away."

Thomas raises his glass high in the air.

"Cheers. So we are so busy in our everyday life back home that we must go to Majorca to be together."

Jesper turns towards him.

"Yes, the world has gone mad as my mother-in-law would have put it."

They get up and walk down the street pointing while looking at all the stores. At a square near the Mexican restaurant they stop to look at a magician who is entertaining the large crowd of people passing by.

The magician stops, some musicians take his place and at once the music begins. They go up to the dance floor and dance to the inciting salsa music while they are laughing and fooling about and are having great fun.

A little later Gitte gets serious again and grabs her purse.

"Excuse me, but I would like to go back to the hotel. I´m exhausted."

Jesper puts an arm round her shoulder.

"Yes, we are out of practice. But perhaps we can meet again tomorrow?"

Thomas who had just seemed disappointed brightens.

"Yes, let's meet by the large stone on the beach next to the Beach Café around 11. Then we can play tennis and have a good lunch together."

They embrace and say good night.

Gitte and Jesper walk back to the hotel where they go up to their room to have some sleep.

First, Gitte calls the number to their own home - no answer. She then rings her mother's mobile number - still no answer. Then she tries her mother's hard-line number - again no answer.

She lies down and looks up at the ceiling. She looks at Jesper who has fallen asleep. She closes her eyes and tries to sleep. But soon after she is again tossing and turning with wide open eyes.

She gets up and once again she tries to ring home without any result. And once again she is restlessly tossing and turning in her bed.

She goes on like that the whole night through.

Chapter 8

Jesper and Gitte are walking hand in hand on the beach. A large clock at a café on the beach is eleven and by the large stone a little farther down the beach Thomas and Vibeke are waving.

When Gitte and Jesper come up to them they can see that Vibeke is grinning from ear to ear.

"Well, sorry, but we are just talking about some people we met yesterday.

We had a nightcap and got chatting with some of the local guys who told us that they have a small eatery behind the Mexican restaurant. One of them lisps oh so awfully.

Well, we are in for a surprise if we go there tonight. You do want to come, don´t you?"

Jesper at once says that it sounds very exciting.

Vibeke looks at Gitte who is very silent.

"Have you still not got in touch with your folks back home?"

Gitte shakes her head.

"Strange" Vibeke says and puts a hand on Gitte´s shoulder.

"Come let´s go back to the hotel then I´ll try to call my mother."

Gitte nods agreement and Vibeke turns towards Thomas.

"Go and have a game of tennis, then we´ll meet here for lunch in about an hour."

Vibeke and Gitte walk back to the hotel along the path.

In the hotel room Vibeke at once calls her mother and Gitte is listening carefully to every word Vibeke utters.

"Hi, mother. Well, we didn´t think we could get in touch after the horrible storm yesterday.

- It has? - We met Gitte and Jesper.

- Yes, it´s great.

- Now, listen ...

Gitte has not been able to get in touch with Inga who is looking after little Markus in their house, you know, on Strandvejen. And now she is getting worried.

- Yes, would you please? And then you´ll call back at one, won´t you?

- Thanks a lot, mom. Bye, bye."

Vibeke turns towards Gitte.

"My mother´s phone has been working all the time, but still something may have happened to yours. Now she´s going down to the house to see if something is wrong."

Gitte thanks her while looking straight ahead of herself.

"But, then, why doesn´t she answer the mobile phone? Surely she must have found out if our telephone is out of order."

She looks as if she´s going to break down any moment now and with a tearful voice she continues.

"One would think that she would then charge the mobile when she knows that we arranged to ring her as soon as we had arrived?"

"Well, yes, but maybe she has forgotten to bring the charger. Come on let´s go along the beach to the tennis courts."

They walk on the beach while Vibeke is trying to turn Gitte´s mind to other thoughts.

"It´s quite a while since we have seen you, but you are very busy, I guess?

Everybody is so busy. Whatever it is they want to accomplish? Does Jesper still work a lot?"

Gitte makes efforts to speak calmly.

"Yes, but we both agreed. Eventually he hopes to be able to delegate more assignments to his employees.

But he has got to be in control of things first. And things develop very fast. As long as his company is so new, we have agreed that he must prioritize things before our family. Later he can always relinquish some of the reins and relax a bit."

Vibeke smiles reassuringly.

"Yes I´m sure that you´ve devised a great plan as you always do. What about you? Do you still work part-time?"

"Yes, it suits me fine that I can have a nice time together with Markus in the afternoon and at the same time it´s also nice to meet other people. And Iben is simply such a great help.

She loves Markus. No doubt about that, but she is also a really nice, sensible and practical girl. The house is always shiny clean and she handles the laundry, too."

"Oh, that´s really nice."

Gitte looks at Vibeke.

"What about you? Do you still teach?"

"Yes, I simply love to teach and I certainly don´t want to do anything else."

"And what about children? Shouldn´t you jump on the bandwagon?"

"Well, we have been talking about it ... many times, but we can't really see how a child would fit into our lives.

I have got my sport - and recently I became a coach for some of the juniors. We're always busy, both of us and besides Thomas travels quite a lot and he's often away for several days."

"But still. I didn't think that I had the time, but immediately after I gave birth to Markus everything else was of no importance. Of course it isn't, but suddenly one is no longer the most important person in life. And then one finds out ..."

Vibeke smiles thoughtfully.

"Well, yes, I suppose so."

Gitte has a nervous look around. Again she takes out her mobile and presses a number. There is no answer and she presses another number.

Again there´s no answer.

Chapter 9

Vibeke´s mother, Susan, goes down to Gitte and Jesper´s house on Strandvejen where she sees that the door is half open. She pushes the door open and goes into the large hall.

"Hello, Inga are you here? Hello! I´m Vibeke´s mother, Susan," she continues. She looks about her and suddenly she clutches her head.

"Oh no."

Vibeke and Gitte are walking on the beach when Vibeke´s mobile rings.

"Vibeke speaking. - Yes, I can hear that. How did it go? - What? No - eh, just a second."

Vibeke turns towards Gitte.

"What´s the number of your mother´s house, Gitte?"

Gitte gapes at Vibeke.

"Was there nobody there?"

"No, but now my mother is going to your mother´s. Perhaps they have gone there to get the charger or?"

"Yes, she lives at number 24, but I don´t understand because there was no answer there either."

Vibeke talks into the phone again.

"Number 24, but don´t tear along, mom.

- Will do. Thank you, mom."

Vibeke and Gitte continue towards the tennis courts where they meet with Thomas and Jesper who look inquiringly at Gitte´s anxious face.

"Didn´t you get in touch with her?"

"No, they are not in, but Susan is going down to my mom to tell her that we would like to talk to her."

They all go round to the small cafe to have lunch. Gitte is quite silent and she is not hungry.

Jesper is watching her.

"Take it easy, Gitte. Has she ever let us down?"

She tries to smile.

"No, she hasn´t."

For a long time the four young people are gazing silently at the sea. From time to time Gitte desperately looks at her watch.

After a while Thomas tries to start a conversation with Jesper.

"Well, well, Jesper, so you are out of practice - who would have thought that?"

"Just you wait. I´ll get my revenge tomorrow."

Thomas goes on.

"It´s the same with Peter. You know, the one I used to play tennis with. It´s as if people stop living when they have children. He has never time to play anymore either."

"It´s not just because of Markus. It´s also the job, you know ... By the way, how are you doing with Danmarks Radio? Are you pleased with your new job?"

Thomas and Jesper go on talking quietly together while Vibeke and Gitte are looking at the sea in silence. There is a strained atmosphere and after a while Gitte turns to Vibeke.

"Didn´t Susan say that they would return the call immediately?"

"Yes, but maybe they are out shopping or something like that."

Vibeke smiles and turns to Jesper and Thomas.

"By the way my, mother sends her regards."

Jesper and Thomas both nod in thanks.

For a moment Vibeke is frowning before she takes grabs her mobile and presses her mother´s number. She places the phone on the table while Gitte is closely watching her movements.

"Doesn´t she answer?"

"No, probably she has put it on soundless, but I´m sure she´ll ring as soon as she knows anything."

Jette Steen

Chapter 10

Susan hurries up to number 24 and on her way she notices an area of sawdust on the sidewalk. She finds number 24 and rings at the door several times, but there is no answer.

A neighbor is raking in the garden next door. She glances at Susan and Susan goes up to her.

"Have you seen Inga recently? Has she gone for a walk with Markus?"

When Susan gets closer she can see that the neighbor is looking solemnly at her.

"Who are you?"

"I´m the mother of Inga´s daughter´s friend Vibeke."

"Well, so you haven´t heard it?"

"Heard what?"

Tears come to her eyes and she takes Susan´s hands as she goes on.

"Inga was run down yesterday on Strandvejen."

Susan is terrified and stutters.

"What about Markus? Was he hurt?"

The neighbor looks surprised.

"I haven´t heard anything about Markus or anybody else, I thought she was walking alone. But Mrs. Iversen next door knows. She was walking on the other side of the road when it happened."

They both hurry up to Mrs. Iversen´s and ring at the door. Mrs. Iversen opens the door and Susan almost scolds her.

"Where is Markus? Was he with Inga when she was run down?"

Mrs. Iversen is very surprised as she asks.

"Who is Markus?"

"Inga's grandchild, she was looking after him."

"No, Inga was alone. I saw it all happen."

Mrs. Iversen is gesticulating while she goes on.

"A large black delivery truck was passing and turned round the corner of Strandvejen where Inga came walking.

I noticed that the driver tried frantically to manueuvre the truck. But eventually he lost control of the car.

The car sped up over the sidewalk and into a tree so that its front was completely wrecked. It almost looked as if the tree had grown up through the roof of the car.

The two young drivers got out and had a dazed look round and on the sidewalk Inga was lying stretched out on her side. She was still holding on to her handbag while a shopping bag and some small bags were lying on the street.

To me it looked as if she was sleeping until I saw blood was running from her mouth.

The two young men went up to her. One of them took out his mobile and phoned while the other one got a blanket from the car which he put over her.

Shortly afterwards we could hear the ambulance and very soon it was there. Inga was placed on a stretcher and with wailing sirens she was taken to hospital.

Soon after the police were there and, well, then I didn´t see more. I was on my way out shopping, you see."

Susan is impatient while Mrs. Iversen is speaking.

"If Markus was not together with Inga then where was he?"

Susan clutches her head and Mrs. Iversen shakes her head as if she doesn´t understand a word.

"Are you sure that he isn´t at home? Or maybe somebody else is looking after him?"

Susan takes out her mobile and calls the hospital.

"From what I´ve understood Inga Meyer has had an accident on Strandvejen yesterday. I take it that she has been hospitalized. Can I speak to her?

- No, I´m the mother of her daughter´s friend.

- Because she´s on vacation. She knows nothing.

- Now, it´s very important that I speak to her.

- But… Yes."

Suddenly Susan rushes out of the driveway while shouting.

"I´m running back to have a look."

Susan hurries down the road, but when she´s going to enter by the front door of the large mansion she finds it locked. She has a look round and walks around the house and the garden.

She looks in through the windows and the windows of the basement and in the small gazebo in the backyard before she decides to go over to ring at a neighbor´s door. Nobody answers the door.

She notices a wide open window at a neighbor opposite and goes over to ring at the door.

When the neighbor, a dishevelled woman about 50 years old wearing an old worn bathrobe, finally answers the door a large brown and savage dog shoots out and jumps threatening up and down.

"Can I help you?" she says without considering the aggressive dog.

Susan is terrified and looks at the dog which at last removes its paws, but still it is growling and remains very close to her.

"Do you know who`s looking after little Markus"?

The neighbor is staring at her with curiousity without saying a word.

"I was here half an hour ago and then the front door was open. I could see there had been a break-in. Have you seen anybody?"

The neighbor glances curiously at the other house.

"Has there been a break-in?"

"Yes, have you seen anything?"

The neighbor now wants to know when it happened and Susan is close to losing her patience.

"I don´t know. But have you seen anybody over there within the past 30 minutes or so? Have you seen Markus?"

The neighbor again looks inattentively at the other house.

"No, I don´t think so."

"Well, thank you."

Susan shakes her head and hurries away.

All of a sudden the neighbor shouts at her.

"Yes, the babysitter came early this morning."

Susan goes back to her.

"Are you quite certain?"

"Yes, I saw her myself."

The four young people are still at the cafe when Vibeke´s mobile rings.

"Now, try to find out ..."

The phone is crackling.

"What do you say? Mom, are you there? Well, now I can hear you again. What was it you asked about?"

Vibeke is looking at the mobile in irritation - it is silent again. The three others are looking curiously at her and Gitte asks at once.

"What was it? Was it your mother? What happened?"

At the same time the phone rings again.

"Hi Vibeke, it`s mom, try and find out where the babysitter lives?"

"The babysitter? Iben?"

"Yes, I think she has picked up Markus."

"No, mom why on earth would she do that?"

"Don´t say anything to Gitte yet, but Inga has been run down. Now, do ask her."

Vibeke turns to Gitte.

"Iben doesn´t live nearby, does she?"

"No, she lives at Bagsværd. Why?"

Vibeke gets up and turning away her face she takes a few steps...

"Mother, Gitte says that she lives at Bagsværd, but why do you think she has picked up Markus?"

"Well, I just spoke with the neighbor. She told me that she saw the babysitter at the house this morning."

"The neighbor? The one with the dog?"

"Yes."

"Oh, you can't count on her. She's raving mad."

"Yes, forget about it. She may also be wrong. I'll call you again when I know a bit more."

"No, wait."

Vibeke suddenly turns around and goes towards Gitte.

"Doesn't Iben sometimes stay over at a friend's?"

"Yes, she has a friend nearby and from time to time she stays over there, but I don't understand? Why?"

"What's her name, Gitte?"

"I really don't understand ..."

"Where does she live?"

"She's called Malene something ... I don't know ... Well, yes, she lives in one of the townhouses, you know ...."

Again Vibeke takes a few steps away from the others.

"She has a friend living in one of the townhouses. Her name is Malene. I really don´t know what you are doing, mom, but do call me as soon as you know something."

"Will do. Take care. I´ll be in touch."

Susan hurries up to ask some people who seem to be locals.

"Do any of you know anything about Markus´ babysitter Iben or her friend Malene?"

The first locals she ask do not know anything, but finally there is a young girl who knows something. She points towards one of the townhouses nearby and says that she has sometimes seen Iben and Malene there and Susan rushes up there.

She rings the bell and the door is opened by a drowsy young girl and she immediately asks.

"Are you Markus´ babysitter?"

"No, it´s my friend Iben who is looking after Markus. Why?"

"We can´t find him."

"No, his parents are on vacation so his granny is looking after him now."

Susan goes on.

"His granny has been run down and I´m afraid that he´s alone in the house. We need to get hold of a key immediately."

Malene grabs her mobile and presses a number.

"Hi, there´s a lady here telling me that Markus´granny has been run down. Do you know where there is a spare key for the house. Wait, you talk to the lady yourself."

She hands the phone to Susan. Iben sounds frustrated when she replies.

"I lost the spare key last week so I handed over my key to the grandmother so that she could get in, but what has happened?"

"Were you at the house this morning?"

"What?"

"The neighbor opposite says that she saw you at the house this morning - were you there?"

"No, I´m at my parents´ in Bagsværd."

"Can you imagine anyone that might have collected Markus?"

Iben breaks into tears.

"Is he all alone ... But that´s awful.

I just can´t imagine who… Do you want me to come?"

"No, there´s no need. Thank you for your help. I got to see what I can find out."

Susan hands over the mobile phone to the young girl and leaves in a hurry. She grabs her own mobile and presses a number.

"Susan Hofman speaking. I can see that there has been a break-in in a house on Strandvejen. Please come at once, I think there is a child in there.

What I know?

- No, I don´t know anything about the burglary, but I could see…

- Is that really necessary? Well. Then I´ll come immediately."

Susan goes home, gets into her car and goes off to the police station. Now she is quite red-faced with her hair every which way.

At the police station she is met at the front desk by a suspicious officer.

"Was it you who called about a burglary?"

"Yes, my name is Susan Hofman."

The officer walks down a corridor and into an office followed by Susan.

"What was it you said you have seen?"

Susan speaks quickly.

"I have just been up Strandvejen at the house, but it was locked. When I was there earlier today the door was wide open and I could see that there had been a break-in."

The officer points at a chair and Susan sits down.

"Were you inside the house?"

Susan looks despaired, but continues.

"Yes, I went in in order to talk to the grandmother who is looking after Markus while his parents are on vacation. But there was nobody there."

The officer looks suspiciously at her.

"And why do you want to go in there again?"

"I´m afraid that the child is in there all alone. You´ve got to let me in there at once"

Susan stutters.

The officer turns a piece of paper and looks at it.

"Excuse me, but who are you? Are you related to Gitte and Jesper Granborg?"

"No, Gitte and Jesper are friends of my daughter´s. They asked me to go down to check, but…"

The officer closely watches the exhausted woman.

"I´m sorry, but I can´t let strangers into the house."

Susan is close to tears and the officer shakes his head while he presses a number on the telephone. Susan is shivering and doubling up as if she is cold as she tensely watches the officer's gestures and the conversation he has just started.

"Johansen, wasn't it you who went up to Strandvejen to lock the house today? - ok, good. There's a lady here who insists that there is a child in the house. Have you seen a child?

- Well, yes, I suppose so.

- No, you didn't, did you?"

The officer turns around and almost gloats as he looks at Susan.

"There was nobody in the house when we locked it up after the burglary."

The officer gets up and Susan shouts.

"But it's a question of life and death. The hospital won't allow me to talk to Inga and if little Markus is in there all alone then…"

The officer is taken aback by Susan.

"What's that about the hospital? And who is Inga?"

Susan explains the matter in detail to the officer who then grabs the phone again ...

Some curious officers walk past the office chuckling as they study Susan.

The officer goes on.

"Yes, the name is Inga Meyer."

The officer looks at Susan who nods.

"Officer Arne Svendsen.

- She is, very good.

- Well, no. What a pity.

- Yes I'll tell her. And thank you very much."

The officer looks solomnly at Susan.

"Inga Meyer is ready to talk to you. You can see her later today. But they said that she doesn't remember anything at all. In the meantime I guess we'd better go to the house to have a look - just to be on the safe side."

Arne Svendsen goes into another office and returns with another officer and then asks Susan to come along. Outside the police station they all get into a police car which starts with wailing sirens.

They stop outside the mansion and immediately after the police officers are opening the front door. They go in and filled with forebodings Susan follows.

As they come out empty-handed after a while the startled neighbors are watching and the officers now begin to question them while Susan grabs her mobile phone.

There are six missed calls and they are all from Vibeke. For a moment she is standing considering in an attempt to find out what to do next.

Chapter 11

The four young people have returned to the lobby of the hotel where they are sitting restlessly looking around them. Finally Vibeke´s mobile phone rings and they all look paralyzed at it.

"Vibeke speaking. Why don´t you answer when I call you? We have been so worried…

- What?

- Oh, no."

Vibeke turns away from the others. She is white as a sheet in her face.

"No, no. It´s not true. I can´t say it… Please talk to Gitte yourself"

Vibeke could not look her in the eyes as she gives the mobile to Gitte who is puzzled as she takes the mobile while trying to establish eye contact with Vibeke.

"What has happened?"

Gitte despairs.

"Will she survive?"

Gitte is screaming, crying and imploring.

"What about Markus?

- No, no. It just can´t be true.

- But it´s awful. Do find him..."

Gitte is dissolved in tears and Jesper who realizes that she is at the end of her tether takes the mobile phone from her. He is nodding and listening to what Susan tells him while Vibeke puts her arms around Gitte in order to comfort her.

"Probably a neighbor has taken care of Markus. Take it easy now. We don´t know anything yet. But it´s awful - the thing with your mother."

Jesper puts down the phone and turns towards the others. He face is ashen.

Gitte is looking at him flabbergasted. Suddenly she screams while she is racing up to punch Jesper´s arm.

"We should never have left without Markus. I did tell you that I wanted him to come with us on vacation."

"There, there - easy now, Gitte. It´s awful, but nobody could tell what might happen. Now we´ll hurry back home and sort out things."

Jesper realizes that Gitte can hardly stand up any longer. He puts his arms round her while turning towards Vibeke.

"Please help Gitte pack her suitcases."

Vibeke seizes her by the arm and they go upstairs.

Jesper and Thomas go to talk to the reception clerk and Jesper´s voice is almost cracking.

"Tomorrow? But we have to leave at once."

The clerk points to a screen while saying.

"There are only two flights taking off before tomorrow. And they are both fully booked."

Jesper is gesticulating a lot while explaining the matter to the clerk and in the meantime Thomas goes up to Gitte and Vibeke in the room.

"There´s no flight until tomorrow."

Gitte breaks down crying while Vibeke puts her arms round her trying to comfort her.

Thomas returns to the reception desk where Jesper cannot restrain his tears any longer. He is sobbing quietly while he leans against the wall.

"It´s my fault. We should never have left until we knew for certain that Inge was with Markus. And now we can´t even get home."

Thomas puts an arm on Jesper´s shoulder.

"It´s no use blaming yourself. You could not know that something would happen to Inga on her short way to your place. Nobody could envisage that."

They remain standing there for a while without anybody saying anything.

The clerk who has been talking on the phone for quite some time now turns around to face them. Jesper dries his eyes and listens carefully.

"Is it true? Are you sure? Oh, thank you very much."

Jesper and Thomas rush off to the hotel room.

"The reception clerk has fixed it so that we can get on the airplane very shortly. We´ve got to hurry up."

Jesper and Gitte immediately get packing while Thomas and Vibeke help carry down the suitcases and bags to the waiting taxi where they give them a hug and a word of consolation.

Chapter 12

Gitte and Jesper are in the taxi. There is a congestion on the road because a procession is blocking the road. The honking cars are running very close to one another and a huge crowd of agitated people are gesticulating and yelling on the road.

Some of them go right in front of the taxi and the driver beeps the horn after which they menacingly knock on the windscreen and lift their arms in a threatening manner.

The driver does what he can to slip past and finally there is a small hole in the angry crowds where he manages to go through. Then he goes on to the airport at full speed where he soon drops them off.

There is a long line at the check-in desk and when finally it is their turn the clerk cannot find their names in the system.

"I´m sorry, but you have no reservation."

"Yes, it was made by the hotel clerk an hour ago ...."

Jesper stubbornly insists and the clerk goes over to a shelving unit and takes a sheet of paper which she closely studies. Meanwhile Gitte and Jesper watches her nervously.

The clerk again logs on the system.

"Oh. Lucky you, here you are."

Finally the clerk hands them their boarding passes and they hurry up to the gate she is pointing at.

When Gitte and Jesper at long last are leaving the airport in Kastrup they look like something the cat dragged in. Their eyes are red, their hair dishevelled and their clothes are wrinkled.

In the taxi they are tense without saying a word and when they reach the driveway of the house Jesper hands the driver some money saying.

"Keep the change."

The very moment the taxi stops they rush out and up to the front door and the taxi driver watches them in surprise while he takes out their baggage and leave it in driveway.

Gitte is crying loudly looking at the empty place in the doorway while Jesper is tearing about the house. Up on the second floor, down into the basement and up again. Then he goes outside where he goes from door to door to talk to the neighbors.

When Jesper returns he sits down into a chair and covers his face with his hands.

"Nobody knows anything."

He leaps to his feet saying.

"Damn, somebody must have seen something!"

A moment later the doorbell rings and Jesper opens the door. Susan is outside with a basket containing a bottle of wine and various food.

"I just want to ask if there is anything I can do?"

Jesper´s shifty eyes look away.

"Well, I guess ... thanks. If you could stay here. Then I think we´ll go to the hospital to see Inga."

Susan goes inside and Jesper and Gitte rush out the door. After a while Arne Svendsen arrives and Susan watches him in a patronizing way.

"Don´t you have any leads at all?"

Arne Svendsen looks at her saying in irritation.

"No, but are Gitte and Jesper not home?"

At that very moment Gitte and Jesper, quite devastated, enter the room. Jesper looks at Susan.

"Inga doesn´t know anything either."

Calling for order Arne Svendsen is gesticulating while looking triumphantly at them before he starts talking.

"We have arrested the burglars. Pure coincidence. I was in a store when I saw Benny buying some cord and…"

Arne Svendsen beckons them to sit down. He himself sits down into a chair and continues his account.

"Benny is just a small-time criminal with a record. Normally just pilfering so I knew he must have an accomplice.

And quite right. Benny admitted that he and a convict called Alex had gone past your house and seeing that the door was open and since Alex had seen you guys leave with your baggage earlier in the day, they just could not help it and they went inside."

Impatiently and slightly irritated Jesper looks at Arne Svendsen.

"Yeah, but what about Markus? Was he there?"

Narrowing his eyes Arne Svendsen again looks as if he is omniscient.

"Yes, they went back to see if you had any booze and then they discovered Markus who was sleeping in his bouncer."

"They got nervous that they might be discovered and then they ran away. But we found all the stolen articles at their place and we keep it all at the station."

Gitte looks at him in desperation.

"But… can it be them? Have they taken… Oh, no."

Gitte breaks down.

Arne Svendsen thrusts out his chin.

"Doesn´t seem very likely that they would take a kid of only one considering all things that would entail. We have left out that theory long ago."

Gitte screams hysterically while looking imploringly at Arne Svendsen.

"Not likely? But we need to find out. How can you just ignore that possibility? We got to go there."

Arne Svendsen looks thoughtfully at Gitte.

"Well, of course I can have an officer or two go there if that will calm you down."

Jesper and Gitte look solemnly at him while he nods.

"The best thing for you to do now is to contact people you know in order to learn if they know anything. Of course, we continue the search and probably there is someone that you have just not thought of who has picked up Markus."

The officer gets up and walks towards the door.

"And try to find some rest. We´ll be seeing you if not before then tomorrow. Bye."

Gitte and Jesper murmur "Bye" and Arne Svendsen walks out the door.

Gitte has brought her mother´s pocket book from the hospital and now she sits down to leaf through it.

"I really don´t know where to start or end. It´s impossible."

Susan and Jesper are looking, too, and Jesper points at a name.

"Who´s Mrs. Iversen?"

Susan at once says.

"Well, it´s one of Inga´s neighbors. By the way, she witnessed the accident. So we can rule her out."

They go on turning over the pages. Despairingly Gitte puts the pocket book on her lap.

"I can´t imagine anybody, can you?"

Susan looks worriedly at her.

"No unfortunately not."

Jesper is pessimistic.

"Neither can I."

Jesper clutches his head. He looks kindly at Susan.

"Well, but thank you for your help Susan. We better see if we can all calm down."

At the same time the telephone rings and Jesper answers it.

"Jesper Granberg speaking.

- Well, you have? Great thing that you remembered, maybe she knows something.

- Yes. - Thank you very much, bye-bye."

Jesper turns and looks at Gitte with a hopeful expression.

"Have you got the number of your maternal aunt, Linda?"

Gitte checks the pocket book.

"Her name is here, but the number is completely blurred - and of course mom knows it by heart. But why?"

"A nurse who was not at the hospital earlier when we were there says that since they could not get in touch with us and Linda had called to inquire, they told her about Inga's condition. So maybe she knows something."

"Oh, Susan, can we persuade you to stay a little longer while we go to see Linda?"

"Sure you can. Get going."

Gitte and Jesper rush out the door.

Later on they walk through the door again and walk into the half-dark parlor. Jesper is pessimistic while entering the parlor.

"Unfortunately she was out. We tried to ring at the door of a neighbor, but there was nobody there either. We´ve tried almost everything."

Jesper switches on the light and in the middle of the doorway Markus is sitting sleeping comfortably in his bouncer. Both Gitte and Jesper rush over to embrace him and tears are streaming down both their faces.

Gitte lifts up Markus looking worriedly at him. She is hugging and clasping him to her and sobbing loudly and Jesper is sighing deeply as he embraces them both and has a look round the parlor.

"How did all that happen?"

Susan emerges in the doorway.

"Linda has just brought him home while you were away."

"Oh, thank God. But has she already left again?"

"Yes, there was a cab waiting for her. But she promised to come back tomorrow."

Jesper walks over to put his arms round Susan.

"Oh, thank you so much for staying here while ....Great!"

Gitte joins them carrying Markus.

"Oh yes, thank you for all you´ve done for us. Just imagine if we had not called you? You have been terrific."

Susan puts on a jersey.

"Oh, I´m only glad that I could do something. But now I think I´ll go home and go to bed. We all need a good night´s sleep. Good night."

The next day Gitte and Jesper are sitting on the floor playing with Markus when the doorbell rings. They both get up and Gitte takes Markus and puts him in the baby bouncer before they go out to open the door.

In through the door goes Linda and she is heartily welcomed. Gitte grabs Linda´s hands and looks inquiringly at her.

"It´s so fantastic that you have looked after Markus. But how did you know?"

"Well honey, I met Inga in the co-op store last week and she told me that she was going to look after Markus while you were on vacation. Then the day before yesterday I happened to meet Mrs. Iversen who told me that Inga had been run down.

I called the hospital to inquire, but nobody knew anything and then I went to your place to see if everything was okay.

The door wasn´t locked and there was Markus quietly sleeping in his baby bouncer. So I took the bouncer, the child and some toys and diapers with me. I have no such things at home.

And then I decided to wait until I heard something from somebody and soon afterwards one of the nurses rang to tell me that Inga had been hospitalized, but that she was not able to talk to anybody.

When I then called the hospital yesterday they told me that Inga was now clear-headed and able to talk and that you had come home and then I hurried over here with him."

With a smile on her lips Linda goes over to look at Markus who is sleeping in his baby bouncer.

"It´s a great invention such a bouncer."

Jesper smiles and puts a hand on her shoulder while pointing at the bouncer.

"Yes Linda, but we don´t call it that. Here we call it a SOLACE SWING."

Jette Steen

ABOUT THE AUTHOR

Jette Steen is a Danish author and she was born only a few houses from where the famous storyteller H. C. Andersen lived through his childhood.

She began writing social realism rather late in life, after a long carrier, due to some unpleasant experiences.

She writes scripts for movies and theatre and has published several books in Denmark.

This is her first book translated into English.

You can see more details on her website: www.jettesteen.dk

www.ingramcontent.com/pod-product-compliance
Lightning Source LLC
Chambersburg PA
CBHW071514040426
42444CB00008B/1645